I0480846

Table of Contents

INTRODUCTION

There are many different options for investing and many types of financial instruments that can be used to accomplish your goal of making profits. One key financial tool that savvy investors and traders use is options.

Almost every other person is afraid of investing the stock market. And since Options Trading is a part of stock market, they don't bother learning about it. Some of them think that stock market trading is some complex process that needs immediate solutions to make big money. While the other people think that it is pure luck, and most of the time people lose money.

Most people are hesitant to invest in stock market because they see other people around them losing money. Not to mention that the people who lose money, barely know what kind of stocks they're purchasing and how they should control the risks and leverage their position.

But the truth is, once you cover the basics of Options Trading, you will learn how to control different assets – stocks, bond or other commodities. You see, in Options Trading, you get an options contract. And within the time frame of that contract, you have the 'option' to either buy, sell, hand over the rights, or just hold on to them. This control over the assets gives you endless choices that can eventually result in more profits. And that's the underlying reason why smart investors choose to invest in Options Trading rather than purchasing the underlying stock. And of course purchasing an options contract is much cheaper than the actual stock, bond or commodity.

As with stocks, options can make a person considerable earnings. They are, however, much more versatile and dynamic than stocks. How so? Well, when trading stocks there are really only two ways to make money. You can go "long" by buying a particular stock and waiting for it to go up in value and if that occurs you can sell it for a profit. The other way to turn a profit is to go "short." In this case, you sell shares of a company and buy them back later at a lower price.

Options trading is much more dynamic with dozens of different ways to make potential profits. Investors can trade options not only on stocks but also on currencies, commodities, and various indices. Many novice investors enter into the stock market without the proper education and experience. These investors are missing out on considerable earnings by not trading options on the above vehicles.

In options trading, you also get to control a number of shares for a lower price. Now that you've got a good introduction of the Options Trading world, let's get you into the Behind the Scenes doors so you can learn how to leverage everything to earn more. To begin with, you will start by learning the difference between the stocks and the options and how they bound themselves. You will also be learning the terms that are used in options trading.

Options are available today on most stock exchanges and can be purchased through low-cost online brokers. Although trading options needs a well thought out and comprehensive approach, you can certainly make a profit if you are dedicated and committed.

Next you will be armed with different strategies that you can choose from time to time to leverage your position, as well as some do's and don'ts that you should keep in mind while trading options. Those are just the basics. And I would recommend you to start by practicing options trading in fake environments (there are websites that allow you to practice that without losing actual money). Or if you are feeling brave enough, you can take on the real world of options.

This book will guide you through the various types of options and strategies involved and, hopefully, allow you to make considerable profits on your invested capital. Understanding options trading is important not only for sophisticated investors but also for beginning traders who want to strengthen their investment portfolio.

Congratulations again for buying my book. Now let us begin!

WHAT ARE OPTIONS

In layman terms, an Option is an agreement that the buyer has the right to transact (the right to buy or sell) the underlying asset at a predetermined price at a particular date. What this means, is that you predetermine the price of the stock that you want to purchase regardless of the fluctuations that occur throughout the period of your contract. Commonly, one options contract equal to 100 stocks of a company.

An option is a contract that gives the purchaser the right, but not the obligation, to buy or sell an underlying asset at a specific price on or before a certain date. An option, just like a stock or bond, is a type of security. It is also a binding contract with strictly defined terms and properties.

Basically, a stock option contract may be in two forms: call options and put options. In both cases you have the right, but not the requirement, to either buy or sell the underlying stock for a predetermined price. The predetermined price is also known as the **strike price**.

An important feature of options, regardless of type, is the expiration date—a date when the option expires and becomes worthless. Before the expiration date, investors can hand over the option to someone else during the month in order to make a profit. However, due to time decay as well as other reasons, the option will lose value the closer it gets to the expiration date.

The attractive part about the options contract is that it binds the buyer and seller into a contract with strict properties and terms to lower the risk of losing.

Consider that I want to buy McDonald's stocks (NYSE MCD) sometime later for instance. The current price of the stock is $101 per share. And judging by their current situation, they are doing pretty well and it is predicted that the stock prices might go up in the near future.

So, I decide to have a call option (it is a type of options contract which will be explained later in this book), and I get the rights to purchase McDonald's stocks at $101.

I decide to buy ten stocks at $101 per stock exactly 60 days from now.

Now that I have the contract, I can wait.

Fast forward to 55 days and I see an increase in the price of stocks. Now, it $200 per share. But because of the fact that I had an option contract to buy 10 shares of McDonald's stocks at $101 each, I could get it at a bargain!

That's the best scenario.

Let's consider a scenario where the price falls.

Consider that instead of the prices rising, McDonald's stocks fall to $50 per share. In this case, my options contract would mean a loss to me, and in no way I would be purchase the stocks at $101 if the current price is $50 per share.

In this scenario, I let the options contract expire and purchase the stocks at $50 per share instead. And that's it. That's all of it. The fact is that you've been trading from a long time without even knowing. Think about the time you were buying your car insurance. It is similar to options trading.

When you bought your car, you got an insurance along with it, just in case something happens. During that time, you had no idea of how much the repairs would cost, nor did you know the price of the car as the time goes on. The price can of course increase, but the insurance will help protect yourself, just in case. Options trading is exactly the same way.

It is a way to give you the ability to purchase a stock at a predetermined rate, and if the price does not increase according to your liking, you can then let the contract expire and then purchase the stock in that company.

BUYING AND SELLING OPTIONS

In option trading, you can either be the buyer or the seller of the option. If you buy a call option, then you have purchased the right to buy the underlying stock (or other underlying instrument) at the specific strike price on or before the expiration date of the option. If you have purchased a put option then you have the right to sell the stock at the strike price on or before the expiration date. In both cases, you can also sell the option itself to another buyer or let it expire.

A different scenario is when you sell, or write, options. In these cases, you are obligated to fulfill the terms of the option contract should the buyer wish to exercise it. So, if you sell a call option, you will have to sell the underlying asset at the strike price to the buyer. And in the case of a put option, you would have to buy the stock at the strike price. If you write options then you need to understand that it is up to the buyer whether or not the contract is exercised and you must be ready to fulfill the terms of the contract. However, it is possible to buy another contract to offset your obligation and in this way you can exit out of the deal.

ADVANTAGES OF OPTIONS TRADING

Once you get a handle on option basics, you will discover that there are quite a few advantages to using them both to increase leverage and to hedge against potential threats.

Leverage

Perhaps the main advantage of options is the ability to make large profits without a considerable amount of upfront capital. This is due to the use of leverage. Financial leverage is one of the most significant aspects of trading in options. This factor can give an investor a bigger return while using a minimum amount of capital in the initial stage of investment.

For example, if you have $1,000 to invest with and you bought stock in company XYZ that is currently selling at $10 per share, then you would be able to purchase 100 shares. If the stock rises to $12.50 you could sell the stock and make a profit of $250 for a return of 25 percent on your initial investment. (For simplicity, we will leave out brokerage commissions in this example.)

In contrast, by buying options on the stock and using leverage your returns could be significantly higher. If you bought call options on the above stock with a strike price of $10 for $10 each, then you could by 100 options which would allow you to buy 1,000 shares of stock. If the stock rises to $12.50 then you could exercise your option to buy the shares at $10 and then immediately resell them for $12.50. In this case your profit would be $1,500 (or a 150% return) on the same initial $1,000 investment.

That is the power of leverage. With options, a trader can make investments without borrowing capital and can control a larger number of shares with a smaller amount of initial investment.

Risk Limitation—Hedging

Another big advantage of options is that they allow investors to safeguard their positions against fluctuations in price, especially when the investor doesn't want to alter the underlying position. In this way, options can be used to protect your portfolio against large price drops. This practice is known as hedging.

Here is an example of how hedging with options can be used as a risk management strategy. Say you own 100 shares of stock XYZ and you are concerned that it may be heading for a fall. You could buy a put option on that stock which would give you the option to sell it at the given strike price, regardless of how far the stock price falls in the market. For the price of the premium, you have insured yourself against any further losses below the strike price. This is a conservative strategy for limiting potential losses in the market.

DISADVANTAGES OF OPTIONS TRADING

It is wise to weigh the potential risks of options against the benefits that may be gained before you decide to try your hand at options trading.

Levels of Risk

There are two levels of risk when trading options depending upon whether you are the holder or writer of the option.

As the holder of the option, your main risk is losing the entire premium that you paid for the option. If the option expires worthless then you are out your entire principal.

As the writer of the option, you are exposed to a significantly higher level of risk. If you are writing uncovered calls, for example, then your potential loss is unlimited as the underlying security could potentially rise very high.

Intrinsic Value

While purchasing a stock gives a certain amount of intrinsic value, with options it is quite different. An option that is currently at-the-money or out-of-the-money has no real intrinsic value. Its only value is its time value, which is constantly declining the closer it gets to its expiration date.

Time Decay

A risk that is unique to options is time decay. The closer an option contract gets to its expiration date the more it loses value. Once the option reaches its expiration date it will have no value unless it is exercised in-the-money. If the underlying security takes an unexpected turn during the timeframe of the contract, the investor will potentially lose all of the investment capital. Unlike with stocks, you cannot simply wait it out. For this reason, options are known as wasting assets.

Taxes

Another element to consider when investing in options is the tax implications of your trades. Since options are short-term investments they are taxed at a different rate than longer term investments. However, losses on options can also be used to offset gains in other investments, so they can work to your advantage in this regard as well. It is best to consult with a tax advisor to figure out your best strategy for tax savings.

The bottom line is that options trading can be used to leverage your positions and make significant profits. However, they come with their own set of risks and require the investor to be constantly on top of what is going on in the market. Due to their unique time constraints, they are not for investors who like to set and then forget their investments.

Parties to An Options Trade

There are 4 kinds of participants to an options trade.

And as common sense suggests, there are buyers and sellers for a particular stock or commodity at hand.

Holders are the ones who why an option. You should not confuse yourself with the terms here (though they are simple to understand). One thing you should always remember, is that when you're holding an option, you "have the RIGHT to buy/sell the underlying stock." For instance, if you are holding an MCD "call" option, you have the right to buy the option at a certain price. And if you're holding a "put" option for the same stock, you have the right to sell it at a certain price.

On the other hand, Writers are the opposite of Holders. They are the ones who sell an option contract. It is obligatory for a Writer to have the underlying stock, or have the cash ready to purchase the underlying stock at a moment's notice.

So for instance, if you're writing an MCD option and decide the on the option type (put or call), the stock price, the expiration date, and the premium (we'll cover that later). You will be giving out THE RIGHT to buy/sell the underlying stock that you have arranged.

In either call or put option, the Holders are not obligated to either buy or sell the underlying asset when the contract expires. This however, is completely different for the Writers. They are obligated to fulfill the terms of the contract.

The Call Option

In a call option, the option holder can buy the underlying asset at an agreed date and price. But the holder is expecting the price of the asset to rise during that time period.

But you should be very careful with this. Because if you, as a holder, buys an asset at an increased price and go along with it, you could end up losing everything. You should remember that once you purchase the asset, there is no cap on how much you can lose. So if your loss continues to increase, your losses will keep increasing.

You should accept the fact that the market is volatile sometimes, and you could go from having everything to losing everything in a snap.

The Put Option

In a put option, the option holder can sell the asset at an agreed price within a certain period of time. A put option is the same as going "short on a stock" which means that you are expecting the price to fall. This means that if the price of the stock falls before the expiration of the contract, you can make a profit.

This can be a good strategy if you know that the stock price will fall after a rise. But you should also know that there is a possibility that it may plateau and not fall at all before your contract expires. The best part about a put option, is that when the price falls, you can earn a lot of profit. But when things go against you, you do not lose money.

So, if you quickly want to turn into profit without having to stick with the underlying asset for a longer time, having a put option is the way to go.

Many investors are looking for the stock prices to fall so that they can make the move. This is because the fallen prices puts them in a leveraging position.

Option Variants

For long term investors, there are option contracts that can be held for many years. This is very similar to the traditional stock market trading where an investor directly invests in the underlying asset.

A plain option is a simple put or call option. While an exotic option may be a simple option, or a completely different option.

Transacting or Closing Out an Option Trade

The reality is that most options are neither bought or sold prior to the expiration date of the contract. A lot of investors simply do not exercise their options.

Sometimes, the option holders sell away their option contracts, while some writers buy back, or hold their own options.

Almost 60% of the options are closed out or traded out, while 30% are expired and become worthless. Only 10% of all the options are actually exercised.

And that is completely fine because there are times when the option's value itself can prove to be profitable enough for you to trade away.

A lot of people find options trading difficult to understand. This is primarily because it is difficult to understand all of its parts.

However, once people understand the science behind options trading, they can eventually harness its art form in order to meet their investment goals. The price of an option is highly dependent on the price of the underlying asset, the volatility of the asset, as well as the remaining time prior to the expiration of the contract. This chapter will go over how the option's price and trade works, and what it means at the core.

The Asset's Price

At the core, the price of the underlying asset is important in options pricing. It's what everything is based off of, and it's the price of the asset. It is what will determine the put and call options as well, and it's what you will be looking at to invest in.

In essence, when the asset price increases, call option prices also increase. However, the put option prices decrease.

On the other hand, if the asset price decreases, then the opposite happens. The put option prices increase and the call option prices decrease. This is to ensure that whatever way it does go, the put and call options follow. If the asset will only be important for a short period of time, commonly people exercise a put option on it. But, if the asset has potential, a call option can be put on it as well.

Because options expire, time is important in option pricing. The longer the expiration time, the higher the option price. As time moves towards expiration, the option price decreases.

That's why it's important to see the immediate gains from it, because an option price may decrease over time, and you might not get the stock for that price ever again.

Volatility

Volatility is also a factor in option pricing. In the case of stocks, those which are stable have lower option prices than those stocks which are extremely volatile. There is also such a thing as implied volatility, which is based on the belief of the market maker. If a lot of people invest in a particular stock, its price will go up. The market maker can adjust the implied volatility to increase the option premium.

As a versatile investment, an option is a cheaper alternative to a stock. Options trading can offer more profits through leveraging. It also limits overall risk. You won't be putting all of your money into one thing, in hopes that it won't fall. Plus, because an option is only valid until the expiration date, your money won't be tied up in it forever.

An investor can only lose money up to the option premium only - essentially what they paid for the option in the first place. Unless if there is a call on it, they won't lose anything else with the option besides the premium, which might be a small price to pay in the case of a stock. Therefore, margin requirements are not required if the investor wants to buy an option.

On the other hand, the option writer must buy or sell the underlying asset if the holder exercised his option. An options writer can keep the option holder's premium money paid - but only if the holder failed to buy or sell the underlying asset before the contract expires. As such, a margin requirement is needed in the part of the writer.

Theoretical Value of An Option

A theoretical value is different from an option premium. As has been discussed earlier, an option premium is paid by the next option holder so that he /she may buy or sell the underlying asset before the option contract expires.

The theoretical value is just an estimate of the present value of the option. It is computed based on the formula of the chosen pricing model. It includes factors like timing prior to expiry, strike price, and price of the underlying asset. Because of the changes these factors undergo during the lifetime of the option, the theoretical value fluctuates continuously until the option expires.

A theoretical value is generated through an option pricing model. Every factor has a certain value and forms part of the theoretical value at a future time. If the stock is chosen as the underlying asset, its theoretical value includes implied volatility, which is based on the option's supply and demand. An investor uses different pricing models to know the option's theoretical value.

Variables like implied volatility, timing, strike price, and underlying asset price are part of the computation. A theoretical value changes over time because these variables also change. A lot of investors and traders use this theoretical value to know the option's value and risk in order for them to make an intelligent decision. Trading platforms also offer updated values while pricing calculators can also be used online.

Using a theoretical formula to determine how much you can potentially make off of an option or stock is important when you're starting out. Using this formula will help give you a good idea of what you'll be getting out of this, and because of it, it'll help you determine whether or not investing in that option is worth it. Knowing the basics of how stocks work, the assets, and what happens to them, you can manipulate the market and get the most for the money that you put into it.

Buying options don't guarantee that the buyer will exercise them prior to expiration. There are, actually, 3 ways to use options.

First, the investor can hold the option to maturity then buy the underlying asset at the agreed price before it expires. Investors do this when the current market price if the asset has gone higher than the strike price.

Second, the investor simply exercises the option sometime before it expires. This is done when the price of the asset fluctuates up and down the agreed price. If the investor believes that the price won't go any higher, he/she can exercise the option immediately after registering a higher price than the strike price.

Lastly, the investor can let the option expire. Investors do this if the price of the underlying asset continuously decline. The loss the investors experience is limited only to the option premium.

How to Sell with Options

Unlike holders, option writers must sell or buy the underlying asset if the holder decides to exercise it. They must buy or sell the asset at the strike price within the agreed contract period - even if the market price of the asset is higher or lower than the agreed price.

A covered call allows the writer/seller to sell the underlying asset which he/she owns. The call writer must sell the asset at the agreed price if the buyer exercises the option. This allows the writer to get all the benefits of the stock as well as the dividends as well. The only time this doesn't apply is when there is an agreement for the person to share the shares that are earned with the stock.

From this though, there is still the issue of the person not fully benefiting from this. They did get the premium and dividend back, but they opted out of any other potential risings in the market, so you should be careful before going into this.

An uncovered call, on the other hand, allows the seller to sell the asset which he/she doesn't own at the start of the contract. The seller stands to lose a lot of money if the price of the underlying asset has risen sharply and the buyer decides to exercise the option. This means that the investor has to buy the asset at a high price only to sell it a loss to the buyer. This can cause a significant loss as a result of the trade, and it can make the person lose a lot of money in the investment as a result.

Watch the Market

It is a common observation that traders allow their options to expire. This is true for traders who trade long positions. The market needs to reach a price to make the option profitable. If a trader wants to consider an option, he/she must look into the probability that the market will reach a certain price. A cheap premium doesn't guarantee a good trade. A good market and potential for that means that it will be a good trade.

You should watch the market for a certain period of time when you are looking into buying a stock option. See the pattern of it, and see if there is a chance for profit with that. If there is, then it's time to go for it. If not, then it might be best to sit that one out and not take the risk with it. You can watch the market by checking the stocks every day and seeing which ones are doing good, and which ones to stay away from.

The Average Monthly Range

A lot of options traders prefer looking at the option premium rather than the possible returns. Although it is important, they tend to focus too much on it, thereby missing the possibility that that the market may reach and eventually exceed the strike price.

In most cases, it is best to keep options trading simple. To decide whether an option is a good trade or not, the options trader can calculate the market's average monthly range. It is a number which offers perspective on the volatility and the possibility of reaching break-even point.

The average monthly range can be compared to other stocks average ranges as well. You might see a stock that has a good trade option, but the average range is terrible and there isn't a chance for profit. However, let's say you see one that's a bit higher than the other, but you notice that there is a lot of potential for that stock. It's better to go with the latter, because it can mean a potential increase in your own profits, and it will end up benefitting you more as a result later on.

Using the Average Monthly Range

To compute for the average monthly range, the trader needs historical prices.

If the stock is chosen as the underlying asset, it is possible to retrieve historical high, low, open, and close prices within a certain period.

The average monthly range needs the daily high and low values of a certain stock.

The average price can easily be computed during the time the market fluctuates between the high and low of a given month. In most cases, conservative traders use the monthly open and close values. The low price is subtracted from the high price during the month to get the range, which is then added up and divided by the months.

[month 1: high price - low price]

+ [month 2: high price - low price] + …

/ (number of months)

(Note: use a spreadsheet or specific calculator/analyzer for this!)

In general, a trader can consider doubling the length of the position to come up with the time frame. Then, it is broken up into 2 time blocks.

Be careful though. This strategy isn't helpful when the implied stock volatility makes the premiums unreasonable. Smaller traders will be forced to buy at outof-the-money strike prices because they don't have enough capital. The average monthly range will tell traders to skip the option trade or use a debit spread strategy in order to be close to the present market price.

The average monthly range can be used in any market at any given time. However, it mustn't be used alone. Market directional analysis must also be used. This concept only prevents options traders from buying cheap premiums with far-out-of-the-money which offer limited returns.

Debit Spread

In a debit spread, an investor buys a higher-premium option and sells a lowerpremium option. Example:

Trader, Bull: Stock F@$10

Buy:	Call:$9/stock	Stock F	100	Prem: $120
Write+Sell:	Call:$11/stock	Stock F	100	Prem: $90

Trader, Bear: Stock F@$10

Buy:	Put:$11/stock	Stock F	100	Prem: $120
Write+Sell:	Put:$9/stock	Stock F	100	Prem: $90

A good benefit of the debit spread is that it offers option traders limited risks and a possibility to get nearer to the present market price instead of purchasing the option outright. The break-even point may also be lower than purchasing an outof-the-money option.

Furthermore, the investors limit their gains in outright option and must be content with a maximum, defined gain. Under some market conditions, this trade may have a favorable trade-off. It will also keep traders grounded on what the market can do.

The promise of unlimited gains is only true when the market moves historically. This is very seldom. Investors who trade for capital appreciation won't stay long if this kind of speculation is observed.

A lot of investors and traders lose money in options trading because they trade options without understanding its ins and outs first.

A solid strategy is needed to profit from the trade. It allows a person to maximize the profit and mitigate the risk. It takes only a small effort to learn how to make use of the power of options and its flexibility.

The Covered Call

The Covered Call strategy allows an investor to buy the underlying asset outright. Then, the investor must write and sell a call option immediately after the purchase on that same asset. The number of shares must be equal.

Example:

Trader:

Buy:		Stock A	100	$10 ea.
Write+Sell:	Put:$10/stock	Stock A	100	Prem: $100

Profit So Far: $100

This strategy is used by investors for their short-term trade and when they have neutral opinion on the underlying asset. It is also used by those traders who want to protect their investment against any possible decline in value. It's a good basic strategy to start out with, and if you're worried about losing out on a possible investment, then this is the way to go.

The Married Put

The Married Put strategy is used when investors are bullish about the price of an underlying asset. They buy shares of the asset outright, and then buy a put option simultaneously of the same number of shares. They do this to protect their investment against possible losses on a short term. It's a way to cash on an investment at the moment, but they don't have to worry about losing anything when the going gets tough. The potential for gains in this is unlimited in a sense.

The married put strategy is like an insurance which determines a floor price in case there's a dramatic plunge in the price of the asset.

Example:

Trader:

Buy:		Stock A	100	$10 ea.
	Put:$10/stock	Stock A	100	Prem: $100

Cost: $100

The Bull Call Spread

The Bull Call Spread strategy is used when investors are bullish over a particular asset and they expect the price of the underlying asset to rise moderately.

They buy a call option at a certain strike price then simultaneously write and sell a call option at a higher price. When prompted, the trader essentially buys the lower-priced asset, then simultaneously sells the higher-priced asset - thus, generating profit.

For this strategy to work, both call options must have the same underlying asset and expiration month.

Example:

Trader:

Buy:	Call:$10/stock	Stock B	100	Prem: $100
Write + Sell:	Call:$13/stock	Stock B	100	Prem: $100

The Bear Put Spread

The Bear Put Spread strategy is used when investors are bearish about the price of an underlying asset. In this case, they expect the price to further decline.

They buy a put option at a particular price, then write and sell another put option at a price lower than their first option. When prompted, the trader essentially sells the higher-priced asset, then simultaneously re-buys the lower-priced asset - thus, generating profit as well.

Like the bull call spread, this will only be successful if investors transact the same asset with similar date of expiration. This strategy limits both profit and, more importantly, loss.

Example:

Trader:

| **Buy:** | Put:$10/stock | Stock C | 100 | Prem: $100 |
| **Write + Sell:** | Put:$7/stock | Stock C | 100 | Prem: $100 |

The Protective Collar

The Protective Collar strategy locks in profit without the need to sell the shares of the underlying asset. Investors buy an out-of-the-money put option, then write and sell an out-of-the-money call option. Again, this only works if investors transact with the same asset.

It is used by investors who go long in an underlying asset and have earned profits from it. If the asset price drops, the held Put option will secure profits. If the asset price rises, you secure profit once someone exercises your written call option.

Example:

Trader: Stock D@$12

Buy:	Put:$10/stock	Stock D	100	Prem: $100
Write + Sell:	Call:$14/stock	Stock D	100	Prem: $100

For new options trader, it is advisable to learn several strategies and improve on making solid returns over time. There are also different things you should keep in mind before you begin options trading. There are mistakes that can be made, but if you're careful and avoid the pitfalls, you will succeed with this.

Here are the top mistakes which the beginner options traders end up making while indulging in options trading. Learning about these mistakes will also help you trade smarter by preventing you from taking wrong actions.

Don't forget to make an exit plan: The first and foremost rule in options trading, just like stock trading, is to control your emotions. Trading in options without having an exit plan can cause you significant losses. Even though options trading seems profitable in the initial stages, it can cause you more loss if you continue to stay in the trade for a longer duration. Hence, you need to have an exit plan for both situations i.e., when you are earning profits and even when you suffer a loss.In order to trade smarter, have an exit plan irrespective of the fact that whether you are buying or selling options. By having a proper exit plan in place you are able to establish a more successful options trading pattern. Have an upside as well as a downside exit plan in place. When you reach the upside positions set by you exit the trade taking your profits. Clear the position if you reach the downside stop-loss.

Purchasing OTM (Out of the Money) Options: Traders, especially those who are new to options trading, end up buying out of the money options. These options are usually cheaper and also popular among traders. The key here that the traders should keep in mind is that the value of the option purchased will decline and hence the option of the contract might either move up or down before the options expiration date. If there is a favorable movement then you can regain the purchasing cost of your options. Though the OTM options are profitable, the profits earned are not consistent. Hence they are not suitable for a volatile market.

Making up for losses by doubling up: There are times when the trade goes opposite of what we expected it to be. In such cases, we tend to forget the trading rules set by us and continue trading with the same option we started our trade with. You must remember that doubling up to catch up rule does not work in option trading. To avoid this mistake and trade smart close the trade when you face losses and look for other opportunities for earning the desired returns.

Overleveraging your option trades: As a beginner to option trading, it is a common mistake to misuse the leverage that is offered by the options contracts. While doing so, traders often neglect the risk factor that is involved in options trading and end up paying attention only to the low cost of options contracts. In order to prevent losses from options trading, understand the leverage well beforehand. The thumb rule is to stick with one options contract in the beginning if you trade in 100 shares lot. This is also considered to be as a good testing amount. In case you fail to get success in these lot sizes, chances are that you hardly will be successful with bigger lot sizes while doing options trading.

Don't be resistant to new strategies: It is often seen that traders opting for options trading, in the beginning, are resilient towards learning new option trading strategies. For instance, many of the option traders say they will either never buy out-of-the-money options or will never sell their in-the-money options. This strategy is absolutely wrong. The best way to prevent losses when indulging in option trading is to understand that options are derivatives. Their prices do not move the same as that of the underlying stocks. Hence, it is essential for traders to be open to learning new option trading strategies. They should learn to cut the trade in order to cut their losses and start finding a different opportunity to make the required profits.

CONCLUSION

While it may seem easier to buy and sell stocks in order to make profits, there are a number of reasons why so many choose to learn options trading. This particular financial tool is complex, yet offers a number of rare advantages that are not available to those trading with stocks.

Trading in options can be one of the easiest ways to become wealthy but that happens only when the traders are able to abide by the basic rules of options trading. As mentioned earlier, options contracts can cause more losses than they generate profits and hence should be a part of the diversified portfolio. Avoid making the above-mentioned mistakes so that you don't end up being trapped in trades that constantly cause losses.

www.ingramcontent.com/pod-product-compliance
Lightning Source LLC
Chambersburg PA
CBHW070522220526
45467CB00002B/810